I0569429

YEAR OF THE DRAGON

poems and meditations on the way

Sunrise Press

YEAR OF THE DRAGON

YEAR OF THE DRAGON

poems and meditations on the way

Ford Turrell

For Mom and Dad

"A bird's free from the chains of the skyway"
　　　-Bob Dylan said that

"Freebird!"
　　　-I said that

Year Of The Dragon (how it started)

And so,

the big door
swings open

to the wall-less house
of possibilities.

There is a Wilder Way

There is a wilder way
    than what we know, *or remember*—
        a way of earth and fire, water and
            air. Maybe you've discovered

this way—or rather,
    had it discover you—
        while you hiked the rocky
            path and felt its sturdy

presence underfoot. Or maybe you
    encountered it as you silently
        sat by the campfire in the black woods
            watching the flames lick at your feet,

reaching for
    immortality.
        Or maybe it pried you open
            the first time you were pinned

under by an ocean wave—
    its total indifference expressing
        your original oneness.
            Or maybe, you felt its

    weightlessness

at the moment you glimpsed
    the red-tailed hawk unfolding
        its noble wings, and leaning,

untethered,

into the empty expanse.

You would be lucky and blessed
        to have received such a message,
                by which you might remember again
                        the beginning—

the undying that forms
        your muscle and blood and bone—
                your wilder way.

Who Does the Sun Shine On?

Who,
does the sun
shine on
at the parting
of the ashen morning clouds?

What being,
is there
to receive
the glory
so freely offered in that moment?

The silent cascade
pours
through
my translucent frame—
I am nothing

but light.

Temple

This morning
I went to the temple
and saw the eye of
Yahweh.
At first, I could not see
It
but then,
after I stopped looking for
It,
and forgot myself,
It
was there,
where
It
had always been—
completely transparent
borderless
and containing all life—
this eye of
Yahweh,
constantly urging us
to finally realize what it means,
"thou shalt not kill"

Low Tide

The benevolent morning light
pulls back the black curtain
of the mysterious night
and reveals—
that the sea has scattered myriad
Treasures
across the beach,
some to return
into the mouth of life at
high tide,
others left behind for dead
in this hard, alien land,
their ancient
beautiful forms—
gelatinous, ridged,
ghost-like, patterned,
tentacled, bulbous, lacy—
each one, our own primordial body,
our water-breathing ancestors,
now imperceptibly
taking their last gasps
in the suffocating salt air
while
beach-walkers
take pictures to
show family and friends.
(Imagine if someone came to make
your portrait while you were
gasping your last).

Why isn't there more
reverence
for these moments,
for this entire earth,
for its numberless beings,
animal and plant,
rock and mineral,
from which we have all
been born,
from which we cannot
ever be separate?

But, this is all just some stupid
poetic, mystic dream of a landscape,
where we respect, and admire, and adore, and
yes—even love—all life,
when the truth is,
we do not even
love ourselves,
and we destroy each other in mass—
with guns and bombs of course,
but also with poverty, sickness, and hunger,
poisons created by the way we have chosen to live,
in greed and ignorance—
and as with our oceanic predecessors,
this very air we breathe is killing us,
and as we gasp
in our collective delusion,
someone has come to take our picture,
and post it on the internet,
and share it with family and friends,
and we think this is good, and

we mostly concern ourselves
with the appearance of
our strange skin bag,
and its bony protrusions,
its waste-filled tubes and bags,
its rubbery pulsing organs,
its electrical currents and
waves of light,
without ever realizing that
this moment in the great unfolding
of evolutionary history
is Life
indifferently (maybe even gladly)
depositing us on the beach
as the
tide
recedes.

Totality

standing
in
the
long
shadow
of
the
moon—

for
a
moment
every
single
thing
is
eclipsed
by
darkness
and
wonder—

a
short
dream
of
a
different
world

Ides of March

Grandpa died
24 years ago
tomorrow.
I was 23 then, he was 78.
Now I'm 47.
He would be 102.
I've been reading about
some Zen masters who lived to be 110 or 120.
I always imagined he would live that long.

He was a cataloger of the world,
an indexer, a student of creation,

and more.

He took photographs of wild flowers during
long walks in the Michigan woods,
and turned those photographs into slides
and labeled them:

Blue Aster (symphyotrichum laeve),

Indian Paintbrush (Castilleja coccinea).

Then he indexed the slides in large shoe boxes.
Sometimes he took out one of the slides
to examine it through a loupe-style
glass that he held up to his eye.
Other times he would project the images
on a large screen in his basement
and study them.

What was he looking for?

He also collected bugs—dead ones. He stored them
in wooden boxes with a clear lid, or
in an old shoe box, sometimes
pinned down and neatly labeled:

            •   •
    Stag Beetle.   *Blue Morpho.*

When I was young, and visited in the Summer,
I would tag along on his wilderness walks, and
we would fish for brook trout in a clear
shallow stream that meandered through the trees,
with just a thin fishing line running through our fingers.

We also filled old milk jugs with ice cold water
that bubbled out of a sun-spotted hillside
rising out of the middle of the woods.

As we walked, he would occasionally stop,

        and consider,

            and share:

            This is a Black-Eyed Susan, he would say, or

            those are Acorn Weevils, or

            do you hear that? that's a Dark-Eyed Junco.

At the time, I was only remotely interested in

these lessons, and I didn't really understand
why he was sharing them with me—I always
wanted to keep moving, to see what was next on
our daily agenda—wondering when we'd get to fish,
or shoot his rifle, or what sandwiches grandma packed for
lunch.

But I   listened.   And I   waited

while he took pictures of these tiniest (but not lowest)
of things that he'd probably photographed
some variation of many times before.

        What was he trying to capture?
        What was he trying to share?
        Maybe nothing.

But I remember him reading a lot—
books, magazines, the newspaper.
He took notes in the margins,
underlined passages,
and scribbled down ideas or questions
on scraps of paper and stuck them
into the folds. After he died, I was in his
den looking at his books and wondering
what to say or read at his funeral. I found
his copy of Thoreau's *Walden*.
In pencil, he had underlined just a single passage—
which begins like this:

        We must learn to reawaken and keep ourselves
        awake, not by mechanical aids, but by an infinite
        expectation of the dawn, which does not forsake us

in our soundest sleep . . . It is something to be able
to paint a particular picture, or to carve a statue,
and so to make a few objects beautiful; but it is far
more glorious to carve and paint the very
atmosphere and medium through which we look . . .

Why did he underline this one passage? What about it
spoke to him?

I wish I could ask him.

Maybe he was just trying to keep himself awake
in this mechanical world—
maybe for him the small, brief lives he catalogued
offered something more.
And maybe he was trying to help us see that too.
To get us to wake up through
all of the glorious details
of these tiny,
perfect,
ephemeral
beings,
each one embodying

the very atmosphere and medium

through which we all exist—

Trillium,
Columbine,
Goldenrod

Yellow Warbler,

Cedar Waxwing,
Thrush

Red Light, Green Light
Act I

Red Light
Sticker on your car window—
cartoon characters
holding assault rifles,
like the kind used to kill children in schools—
Why?
Green Light

Red Light
a mother leans in,
and tenderly kisses her two small
children on their foreheads,
then she turns to go—
they part,
but she knows
they can never be apart—not ever
Green Light

Red Light
shaped like Buddha,
draped with strips of
brightly colored fabric,
dotted with a kaleidoscope
of beads and jewels dangling
from strands
of wire and string,
your small cart,
like a pot of gold
at the end of the rainbow,

brimming
with mysterious radiant treasures—
you see me,
and smile
like Buddha.
Green Light

Striving

one day,
i'll stop all this striving—

    and that will be a relief

For Once

just look
at your tired eyes
in the mirror
for once
without
judgment

Other People's Me

Isn't it strange
how the measure of our own
self worth
rises and falls based on the
opinions
of other people,
each harboring their own
neuroses,
each carrying their own
resentments,
each bearing the weight
of their own
histories and
traumas?
We suffer at a word,
a look, a silence.

Why do we do that?

We need to
realize
that how other people
perceive us
is a clearer
reflection
of them
than of us.

Why construct
an image of *yourself*

based on how other people think
about *themselves*?
Why allow them to have
that kind of influence?

Your true self is not what other people say
        or think about you.
Your true self is not subject to anything outside of you.
Your true self is stainless.
Your true self is boundless.

Real Peace

If your deepest wish
is to taste real peace,

watch the freckled loons
diving on the cold black
lake in the glassy morning—

gliding effortlessly,

then
gone

in one motion,
then
reappearing
somewhere else,
content
just to be doing
what they do,
nothing extra,
nothing lacking—

>   nothing extra,
>   nothing lacking

Relief

It's so dark

        at night

in the mountains

      and then

           light

floods into the valley

Red Light, Green Light
Act II

Red Light
five gray and brown sparrows
swiftly descend
and encircle
several white grains
arranged on the sidewalk—
chattering and taking turns
at breakfast
Green Light

Red Light
a ring of bright orange cones
surround a fresh, deep gash in the violated earth—
they declare:
"WARNING! Someone has killed many beings."
Like mourners, they peer
into the dark grave of progress
Green Light

Red Light
a tall man
in a navy blue suit
talks seriously
with a another man
near the courthouse steps—
the other's face contorts
like he's just seen the devil
Green Light

The Hunter

The hunter comes
on eagles wings,

raven black
in the icy sky,

then a sudden flash of white
from the tail—

like Cortez sailing under
the blood-red standard that

flickers

between leaden swells
through the centuries,

as he silently
cuts his way across the sea—

killing on his mind—
a fleet of caravels,

there, in the scan,
can you see them?

1

distant thunder
like careening boulders—
the wide-eyed Robin shits on the fence

2

old pine fencepost
weeping sap
it's alive!

3

the butterfly
rests on the lilac—
sharing the briefest of lives

4

white hydrangeas
piled on the bush—
spring snowballs

black sabbath

From the outside,
the house is dark

and inside—

The kitchen dark
The bedroom dark
The shower dark
The faces dark
The breakfast dark
The sunlight dark
The dog dark
The mind dark
The chatter dark
The laughter dark
The nausea dark
The motions dark

it was
Saturday,
or was it Sunday?

black sabbath

War Chief

This life of peace,
the clearing left
in a path of great violence

The war chiefs
venerated
for making peace

This is our history
like it or not

This is where you sit
like it or not

Blood on your hands—
while making dinner
while washing the dishes
while rocking the baby

So Much Depends

so much depends
upon

belief in a
self

totally separate from
others

in order to
kill

Gulls

From the other side
of the dark expanse,
a large flock of gulls,
lost
somewhere
between land and sea,
unseen but heard,
their shrill cries
a ricocheting cascade
skipping across
dawn's great empty room—

like the howls
        of grief,
the wails
        of displacement,
the shrieks
        of rage,

repeatedly echoing
through the
great empty hall
of human history.

Revelation

morning breeze
dissolves the mist—
reveals
world in spring
ah

The Path

There is only one path—
and it is this very moment
this one

Evergreen

A solitary beacon,
I have wanted to write you for a long time,
blazing amidst the stalky brown winter maples
entrenched in deep snow,
a towering sentinel
watching over me—
the hands on the clock
spinning away life's hours—
worrying about this   and   that
striving for this   and   that,
grieving this   and   that.

and long after I stop returning,
when my tired body no longer marks the hours,
and the pendulum of my breath hangs motionless,
there you'll be,
nested on the wooded bank of the pond,
encircled by the skinny poplar and the shrubby scrub,
watching the geese come and go with the seasons,
turning toward the the fresh wind,
warming in the morning sun,

like we used to

The Heron

The small fishing boat has
nearly vanished
in the smoky mist
that swirls up
from the dark water;
flocks
of ducks
and geese and swans
slowly swim out
from their nighttime coves,
from their hiding places
among the reeds;
safe now, they emerge
with the coming light,
brightening, as it does,
in the eastern sky,
orange, yellow, purple, blue;
wisps of pink clouds,
like floating feathers;
a dream.

What is it to be alive?
To see these sights?
To have this body?
Is there a way
in which
the one who sees
is the same
as what is seen?

A tall heron
stands motionless
in the shallow water;
it is not hunting;
it is wholeheartedly
watching the sun rise.

M.J.O.
  +
M.M.C.

How could I say anything
you haven't already said,
so completely, so flawlessly—

even your initials,
carved deep
into the ancient pine,
standing in its 'dark peace'
beside the vast ocean,

bring me eternal comfort.

Gently, Gently

Standing
in the icy wind,
staring
at the orange creamsicle
horizon,
the sun
came
slowly and gently—
easing
herself
into this brand new world
again.
As if to say, "slow down,
take it easy, take it in."

Same, Same, Same

failure
      green tea
fear
      morning window
anger
      sleeping dog
despair
      birdsong
self-hate
      candle flame
panic attack
      children laughing
disease
      green forest
grief
      ringing bells

same, same, same
same, same, same
same, same,

      same

Real Love

Real love
is not
something
you
can control,
or
keep,
or even
hold onto.

Real love
is
something
that
holds us,
and
everything else—
eternally.

Quilt of Life

In the first pink light of morning,
the large flock of geese
simultaneously
rose from the dark, still lake
beating the life drum,
splashing the black water,
pulling themselves from the invisible seam—
and
in their wake,
out from the churning sparkling cauldron,
all life flowed,
as from a great spring,
a single river, rising
up, and out,
as the midnight water,
the shadowy pines,
the powdery sky,
the cottony clouds,
the solitary figure—
all flowing and changing—
the billowing flag of creation in every direction,
the quilt of life in the vast cradle of the universe.

Red Light, Green Light
Act III

Red Light
sunrise
tall black man
bright yellow terry-cloth robe
brilliant white fluffy slippers
black knit hat
gliding
as though a breeze
through the crosswalk
Green Light

Red Light
autumn leaves
wildly scurry
and gust
through the empty intersection
like dozens of
frantic children
running from bombs
in Ukraine
and Gaza
and Israel
and Lebanon
Green Light

Red Light
this intersection, a
woodland clearing—
chattering voices

the chickadee,
semi-truck air brakes
the crow,
traffic hum
the river, the wind, the rain
Green Light

Hopelessly Hopeful

It's so easy to feel hopeless sometimes
what with, all the people killing other people,
and the politics of power and greed and hate
that get sold to us like a used car as
"fundamental to democracy",
words so stripped of any meaning
they might as well be on the menu at Starbucks or
McDonalds—"cheeseburger", "democracy".
What with, all the people in this world
without enough food,
or clean water, or basic care or medicine.
What with, species going extinct because
we destroy their habitats to
make processed foods and plastics that cause
cancer, and dementia, and pollute the oceans—
just to make more money,
but we somehow ignore all that
for the convenience of it all.
Sometimes the view is bleak.

It's so easy to feel hopeful sometimes,
what with the big warm dog laying at my feet,
the rows of pink and white and yellow
flowers turning their faces to the sun in the garden,
the ripening plump tomatoes hanging
near the wooden fence,
my children soundly sleeping upstairs,
the birds, the birds, the birds, who sing
and cheep and chirp every morning because
they are alive, and not dead in the road, or killed by a hawk.

What with, all the caregivers changing
soiled sheets in hospitals and hospices,
the teachers holding little hands and
teaching children to read and write,
the artists trusting the truth pounding
in their hearts just enough to push through
the fear that they will fail or be judged.
Sometimes the view is blue sky.

Herons

A pair of herons,
paddling their way
over the branchy treetops,
with their strange geometry,
their cardboard bodies
shaped to hold
a basket of trout.

Carry It With You

You carry
this world
with you
wherever you go.
Like a pack
on your back
only
it's all around you
just kind of
riding along
but appearing
now
for the first time—ever.

And you along with it—

The gentle scrape
of the tea cup on the saucer.
Brown-green moss
on the garage roof.
Smell of wood smoke
in the blue morning.
Your face
in the mirror.
The rise and fall
of your breath—
        gathering in   then releasing.

Sky Spider

It seems like it would be a bad idea
to climb your bitsy body
up thirteen stories
to build your fragile home,
completely exposed
to the wind and the rain and the sun and the birds.

What drove you to this place?
Is it overcrowded at street level?
Every nook, cranny, window corner,
street lamp, and park bench
already occupied?

In the morning, your delicate
woven framework is perfectly
strung with shimmering water beads,
each one a reflective orb
containing the entire sky.

Did you do it for art? Is this
just a display of your
mastery of design and geometry
and physics?

Usually you are nowhere to be found,
like you spent the long night working
but skedaddled before dawn—Picasso
spray painting the freeway overpass.

By afternoon, the elegant strands have stiffened,

dried by the wind, baked in the sun.
For hours the entire lattice
pulses in the gusty wind.
Somehow, only a few sticky corners
attach the entire thin frame to the giant building.

       Is this your ancestral hunting ground?
       Like an African lion born on
       the drought-ridden savannah?
       Certainly, there are bugs in less
       hostile places—like my backyard.

As the sun sets, some of the threads
have torn away, the intensity of the sun and
the pressure of the wind is too much.
They wave freely over the
cars and people far below—and
so it is with us too sometimes—our threads
detach and flap freely in the wind and we
barely hang on.

But by dawn,
everything
will be back in its place.

And what about me
up here
spinning
my own clumsy web (or maybe
just caught in one),
so far from, and yet somehow
still part of, the great earth
from which we have both come.

5

broken pen—
ink still flowing

6

this perfect morning,
the blue sky
filled with anxiety

7

a million shimmering galaxies
wind in the leaves

8

this sickness
strikes me down—
total well being

The End of the Dream

Tossed
upon the
fathomless sea
of the long night,
urged
along by
the invisible winds
of a synaptic fantasy,
you flail and stumble,
grasping
at this and that—
the pillow, the sheet,
another person, perpetually
conjuring
your own existence,
projecting
images on the wall of
the cave,
hieroglyphs—
is this me? is that me?
To truly know,
you have to die at the end of the dream—
by and by,
the perpetual dawn
calls us (home),
its ancient light
revealing
all as transparent—
here and not here.
Awed,

you still, then
you stir,
and awaken
into the dream—

opening your eyes,
the whole world
flickers
into existence.

**hate, hate
(for a friend)**

hate, hate
double-helix
DNA of human suffering
shared by one, shared by all

community of discord
fellowship of pain
divided mind—
        still one

lineage

a new sapling,
its thready roots
reaching through the darkness,
unites
with the vital source
of its encircling ancestors,
across
generations, kind, and classification,
they share—
light, water, air,
fire, drought, flood—
though seen as several,
in the deep vast loam,
they uphold one body,
one lineage,
for all

Hurricane Season

There once was a place called Florida,
a "place of flowers",
a botanical beauty,
always rumored to contain the
fountain of youth,
where people flocked
to be revived, to lengthen their lives.

Its first foreign seeker was
killed by the native foliage—ironic;
Its second seekers were
engulfed
by the boiling seas, which
swallowed the blooming peninsula
in one gulp.

It sounds like an ancient myth,
but it's not. The place of flowers,
is now part of the sea floor;
there's whole cities down there;
gardens of rust,
blossoming buildings and bridges over
dark cavernous causeways lined with quiet cars.

Silent sanctuaries for the
bright clown fish,
the slimy eel,
the giant squid.

Reprise
(There's an eel in my SUV)

There's an eel in my SUV
With one jolt it can charge the battery
If only we had someplace to go
And weren't sunk 1,000 feet below

Geese

One flock goes east
One flock goes west
        -headed in the same direction

Rest

Walking in the woods this morning
after a cold front pushed through overnight.

The trees don't stop moving in the fresh breeze.

Their leaves—
like running your hands through
smooth coins in a treasure chest.

Just walking,
all things are at rest.

Numbered Days

All the little summer insects
living numbered days until
the first frost—
Are they afraid?
Are they fretting the day
the cold silently extinguishes
their tiny lives?
No!
They're all just
Buzz   buzz   buzz
right up to the end.

First Snow

Last night, as I tried for sleep,
the first real snow of the winter fell.
Everyone was tucked into the deep quiet that
only snow can bring.

My body hummed with the reverberating silence.
I thought of the people I knew who were
in their sick rooms—

> one in the hospital, lungs filling with fluid;
> one at home, veins rippling with chemo-poison;
> one upstairs, body trembling with fever.

Yet, this new, spotless
blanket of white,
made up of innumerable, singular crystals,
fell into place gently, like a cool hand to the forehead;
tenderly covering this entire ailing world—
this world where most
suffer terribly in the shadowlands between
nebulous borders—
discarded anonymous sacrifices for power and dominion.

And yet,
every heart knows—
if you ask deeply enough,
that there are no borders
separating
any of us—not one.

And that, in truth, we are all gathered together
in one sick room, and it has no walls,
and that I see and feel the suffering
of all people and all creatures in every
corner of this world—and you do to—
if you ask deeply enough,
and you

      just listen; and

         just trust

the resounding silence holding us all————

this heavy heart

the path is
one emptiness
arising just now
as
stress from work
anxiety about a sick loved one
pain in the upper back, or the left hip
fear about the future
regret about the past

but the path has no future
the path has no past
the end of the path is here
right now
the beginning of the path is here
right now
dishes clanking in the kitchen
airplane overhead
smell of the pine candle
this heavy heart
this heavy heart.

Sign on the Door

The sign on the door reads:

In these few brief moments,
let us just accept ourselves
completely,
with our wild mind,
and our defenses,
and our regrets,
and our pain,
and our anxiety,
and our negative self-talk,
and our desire,
and our anger,
and our fear—
Let us just allow all of it
to appear and be here
for now,
as part of the whole,
as it all comes,
nothing lacking,
just part of the whole,
not to hold it,
not to cling to it,
not to judge it,
just to welcome it,
as it is,
for now.

9

lined up on the roof peak
waiting out the rain—
patient pigeons

10

ahh
this Way—
who knows?

Why I Run Barefoot In A Grassy Field

because the grass
because the wind
because the leaves
because the red-tailed hawk
because the whitetail deer
because the heron
because the geese
because the maple and the oak
because the birdsongs
because the soft earth
because the sky—

because the more I go,
the more I see and
hear and feel;
the more I am a child again,
in wonder,
in awe, back to
the beginning,
before I knew,
before I shut myself off,
before I closed myself in, with
my rational mind and my
irrational fears;
before I believed
everything was separate from me,
separate from my elemental body;
back to a time when
my heart leapt at
roiling clouds, rolling thunder, and

first drop of rain;
back to a time when
my heart moved toward
the blazing orange dusk, the empty moonlit lake,
my mother's young face;
back to a deeper connection with
everything that was, without question,
a part of me, but
now isn't me,
until it is
again,
when I run barefoot in a grassy field.

Returns

Today,
      the great earth
         reached
            the apex of
               its slow roll
                   away from the sun,
             and now we start
          the gentle return
       from the cold dark
    to the warm light.

There is planted
      in each of us
         a little seed
            of longing
               to return,
                   to some other time,
               some other place,
            some other feeling,
         than this one—a sense
      that we need to be restored
from our current condition,
      that we are not whole,
         that part of us
            always remains
               in the cold, dark.

But today,
      when I saw
         the golden pearl

of the dawn sun
              setting fire to the clouds
                          and the water
              and the bare trees,
          and I felt the warmth
      of its flames
    on my face,
this seed
    again
          cracked open
            and then
                  completely dissolved,
                            because I
              remembered that
          what I longed to
        return to, what I
    believed myself
estranged from,
      what I convinced myself
        I lacked, was already here,
              and always had been here,
                  ripening in the cold,
                      and in the dark.

Year of the Dragon (how it ended)

The true dragon has no end—
its body stretches beyond
any conceivable time or horizon,
an iron sea,
from which our lives
miraculously blossom and bear fruit,
pure love,
always present,
waiting to cut through our
delusions, and ignorance, and greed,
if we could just let it,
if we can just let go enough
of all that we cling to,
just let go enough
of this self that walls us in,
just let go enough
to let it be exactly what it is in this moment,
now breathing fire,
now freely sweeping across the sky,
now sleeping in the mountains.

YEAR OF THE DRAGON

poems and meditations on the way

Ford Turrell
Sunrise Press

Acknowledgment

The author would like to acknowledge and honor that the year of the dragon is part of the traditional Chinese calendar and zodiac, and an important part of Chinese cultural tradition. This collection of poems was composed during 2024, a dragon year. The author was also born in a dragon year, and in the most profound way, this collection arises out of a felt connection to this ancient symbol of transformation, connection, freedom, and the universal, among other things. If this is in any way taken to be a misrepresentation or mischaracterization of this ancient and beautiful symbol and tradition, that is not the author's intention and the author sincerely apologizes.

A Note About the Author

Ford Turrell lives in Michigan. This is his second book of poems and meditations.

For more information, or to book an event, contact:
sunrisepress3@gmail.com
@fordturrellpoems
https://fordturrellbooks.com